Original title:

From the Ashes

Copyright © 2024 Swan Charm

Author: Kätriin Kaldaru

ISBN HARDBACK: 978-9916-79-081-6

ISBN PAPERBACK: 978-9916-79-082-3

ISBN EBOOK: 978-9916-79-083-0

Enkindling the Unthinkable

In the shadow of silence, dreams start to spark,
Whispers of hope in the depths of the dark.
Visions awaken, like flames in the night,
Casting away gloom, igniting the light.

Hearts beat in rhythm, a dance of the brave,
Sailing through chaos, the uncharted wave.
Fears become embers, that flicker and fade,
Fueling the fire of choices we've made.

Through valleys of doubt, we journey and roam,
Finding our way, through the vastness of foam.
Every step taken is a story retold,
Of courage and strength that ignites the bold.

Hands lift the weight of the world on their backs,
Transforming the burdens into vibrant tracks.
Beneath the dark sky, we'll rise from the ground,
With dreams that unshackle and joy that is found.

United in purpose, we echo the call,
For every heartbeat is a spark, after all.
In the heart of the storm, let passion unfold,
Enkindling wonders, both silver and gold.

A Canvas of Charred Hopes

In twilight's breath, ashes fall,
Dreams painted bright, now dimmed and small.
The canvas rests, a tale unfolds,
Of fire and loss, and courage bold.

Yet within the embers glow,
Fragments of visions begin to show.
From charred remains, we seek to find,
New colors to fill, and reshape the mind.

Each stroke of loss, a lesson learned,
In the light of sorrow, resilience burned.
With each defeat, we rise anew,
A canvas reborn, with brighter hues.

Dreams Reignited

From ashes deep, a spark appears,
Whispers of hope replace the fears.
In shadows thick, a light will grow,
Dreams once lost, now start to glow.

Through the night, a path unfolds,
A story of courage that time has told.
With every breath, we stake our claim,
Reigniting dreams, igniting flame.

The past may haunt, but we hold tight,
To visions born from darkest night.
With hands outstretched, we reach for more,
In the dance of dawn, we soar.

The Echoes of Incendiary Nights

The stars bear witness to the fire's gleam,
Echoes whisper secrets of a fevered dream.
In the heat of chaos, our spirits rise,
Burning bright under the moonlit skies.

Flickers of passion in the midst of fight,
Each flame a story, a heart's delight.
In the aftermath, we seek to mend,
The echoes remain, and we transcend.

From embers cooled, our voices sing,
A symphony of hope that joy does bring.
Together we'll stand, in memory's embrace,
As the echoes linger, lost in space.

Glistening in the Dark

When shadows creep and silence reigns,
Hope glistens softly, breaking chains.
In darkest depths, a spark ignites,
Guiding the way through lonely nights.

With every heartbeat, a promise made,
The glimmering paths through fears we wade.
In the cloak of night, we carry our dreams,
Shining like starlight, bursting at the seams.

Finding our strength in the depths we tread,
Glistening visions of the life we've led.
Through trials we rise, together as one,
In the dark we shine, til the morning sun.

Rebirth in the Flames

From the ashes, life anew,
Flickers bright, a vibrant hue.
Hope ignites where shadows fade,
In the fire, our dreams are made.

Wings unfurl, the phoenix soars,
Through the heat, we open doors.
Crimson glow, a sacred dance,
In the flames, we take our chance.

Rising high, no longer bound,
In the inferno, strength is found.
Cleansing heat, we shed our fears,
With each spark, we dry our tears.

Embers whisper tales of old,
Of battles fought and stories told.
In the blaze, we find our way,
Rebirth brings a brand new day.

Fires fade and light transforms,
In the heart, a new life warms.
Through the blaze, we rise anew,
In the flames, we find our true.

The Ashen Horizon

Beneath the sky of muted gray,
A landscape marked by yesterday.
Where ashes fall like silver rain,
In the stillness, beauty's pain.

Fragments of a world once bright,
Scattered under fading light.
Yet in the dusk, a promise gleams,
Hope reborn within our dreams.

Silent echoes, whispers low,
Guide us gently where to go.
Among the ruins, life will strive,
In the ashes, we revive.

Every breath, a brand new start,
In the dust, we warm our heart.
Color seeps through barren ground,
In the ashen, life is found.

Horizons stretch, a canvas bare,
With gentle strokes, we start to care.
From shadows rise, we take our place,
In the ashen landscape, grace.

Eclipsed by Ember's Light

In the dark, a flicker stirs,
Softly dancing, light obscures.
Eclipsed by shadows, yet they glow,
In the night, we come to know.

Embers flicker, stories past,
Whispers of the light amassed.
In the silence, warmth remains,
Filling cracks, healing pains.

Veiled by smoke, the stars do hide,
Yet within, our hopes abide.
From the chaos, brighter beams,
In night's arms, we weave our dreams.

Beneath the glow of fading fire,
We find amidst the night our desire.
Light will rise through trials faced,
In ember's heart, we stand embraced.

Eclipsed not by the darkened sky,
But by journeys where we fly.
In the depths, the light will break,
From ember's touch, we wake.

Renewal of the Scorched

Fields once charred, now whisper green,
Nature's art, a vibrant scene.
Scorched and bare, but life will spring,
In the stillness, hear hope sing.

Beneath the soot, the roots entwine,
In dark soil, the world's design.
From every fall, a rise is found,
Renewal waits beneath the ground.

As the sun breaks through the gray,
Waking life, the dawn of day.
Burnt remains become the soil,
From the ashes, dreams uncoil.

Life reclaims what once was lost,
Every victory, worth the cost.
In the warmth of sunlit skies,
A resurrection never dies.

With each cycle, lesson learned,
In the fire, our strength returned.
Scorched remains, a promise true,
In renewal, we bloom anew.

Flourish from Ruin

In the ashes, new life stirs,
Hope emerges, as darkness blurs.
Roots entangle in broken stone,
From the fragments, strength has grown.

Silent whispers of the past,
Echo through the stillness cast.
Beauty blossoms where it fades,
Resilience found in nature's shades.

Through the cracks, the flowers break,
From the sorrow, new paths make.
Each petal holds a tale untold,
In every hue, brave hearts unfold.

Rising high from jagged ground,
In the chaos, peace is found.
Embers warm the chilling air,
From the rubble, hearts lay bare.

So let the past lay down its weight,
In every failure, there's a fate.
From the ruins, let us grow,
In a garden where hope will flow.

Daring to Ignite

When the spark is barely seen,
Dare to reach beyond the screen.
In the stillness, passion waits,
For the moment, love creates.

In the darkness, flickers dance,
Inviting chance, a bold romance.
Set your dreams to skies so bright,
Daring hearts will find their light.

With every fear, a chance to rise,
To paint the stars across the skies.
Each heartbeat a beautiful song,
In the courage, we belong.

Fire's glow in every gaze,
A quiet warmth in longing's blaze.
With each touch, the night ignites,
In the shadows, love excites.

So let us dance through midnight's glow,
With every step, our spirits grow.
Embracing all that lights our way,
Daring to ignite, come what may.

Shadows Blossoming

In the dusk, where whispers sigh,
Silent blooms learn how to fly.
Petals folding, gently curled,
In the shadows, beauty swirled.

With each heartbeat in the night,
Softly hidden from the light.
Nature thrives in quiet grace,
Finding strength in dark's embrace.

Mysteries of the twilight bloom,
In the depths, dispelling gloom.
Silent songs that softly rise,
From the shadows, hearts devise.

Every leaf, a secret keeps,
In the silence, wisdom seeps.
From the dark, bright colors flow,
In the night, the shadows glow.

So let the petals bloom away,
In the night, they'll find their way.
Through the dark, know you will find,
Shadows blossoming, intertwined.

The Rise of Celestial Cinders

From the stars, we come to gleam,
In the cosmos, we dare to dream.
Celestial fires light the way,
Guiding us to a brighter day.

Though the tempest may rage high,
In the chaos, we learn to fly.
With each spark, a story spins,
In the dance where the journey begins.

Cinders glimmer, hope ignites,
Filling hearts with endless lights.
In the depths of the universe,
Every flame, a whispered verse.

As we rise from ashes gray,
In the night, we find our play.
Connected through the cosmic thread,
By the light, we are all led.

So let the stardust form a guide,
In the cinders, we shall abide.
In the vastness, let us soar,
The rise of celestial cinders, forevermore.

Transformation's Embrace

In the twilight's tender glow,
Through shadows deep and low,
A heart once lost, now finds,
The strength that love unwinds.

With every breath, reborn,
The weary soul, now worn,
A dance of light ignites,
Emerging from endless nights.

The whispers of the past,
Fade gently, fading fast,
With courage, we ascend,
To realms where dreams transcend.

Fragments of the broken,
In strength, the unspoken,
Rise like flowers from ash,
In beauty, we will clash.

Together, hand in hand,
We craft a brighter land,
In transformation's grace,
We find our sacred space.

Rising Embers

Beneath the cooling sky,
Where weary spirits lie,
A spark begins to glow,
In silence, life will flow.

The night may seem so long,
But hope sings a sweet song,
In darkness, embers gleam,
Awaken from the dream.

Each flicker tells a tale,
Of courage, love, and frail,
The fire learns to rise,
Reaching for distant skies.

With ashes left behind,
We seek what's undefined,
Through struggles, we will find,
A pathway intertwined.

Through rising embers bright,
We venture into light,
For in each heart ablaze,
A journey we will praise.

Phoenix of Hope

From down below the ground,
A whisper, gentle sound,
A flame begins to soar,
To open every door.

Its wings spread wide, a sigh,
As dreams begin to fly,
Through trials, burned and frayed,
A brighter path displayed.

Through ashes we arise,
Reflecting in the skies,
The warmth of courage shared,
In hope, we find we're spared.

The phoenix sings a tune,
Beneath the crescent moon,
In every heart it dwells,
A secret that compels.

So let the world ignite,
Our spirits taking flight,
For in the flame's embrace,
We find our sacred space.

Whispering Cinders

In soft and silent night,
Where cinders hold their light,
A story seeks its voice,
In shadows, we rejoice.

The embers glow like stars,
In perfect, sacred jars,
They whisper of the past,
Of moments meant to last.

Each flicker sings of dreams,
In laughter, love redeems,
While memories take flight,
In radiance of night.

With every shifting breeze,
The heart finds its release,
In whispering cinders bright,
The hopes of endless light.

So gather 'round the flame,
And cherish every name,
For in the warmth, we see,
The bond of you and me.

Reawakening the Spirit

In the stillness of dawn's first light,
Whispers of hope take joyful flight.
With each breath, the world renews,
Heartbeats echo ancient views.

Beneath the shadows, dreams arise,
Dancing softly, like fireflies.
Every moment, a chance to grow,
Nurtured by the love we sow.

Through the trials, we find our way,
Guided by the break of day.
Each step forward, firm and free,
Unveiling what it means to be.

In the stillness, the spirit sings,
Finding joy in simple things.
With every laugh and every tear,
We embrace the magic here.

So let us rise and lift our eyes,
To greet the sun and touch the skies.
For deep within, a flame is stoked,
Reawakening the spirit, evoked.

Scattered Remnants Reclaimed

Upon the ground, the echoes lie,
Fragments lost to days gone by.
But in the heart, a spark remains,
A journey through forgotten pains.

With gentle hands, we pick and choose,
Gathering tales we cannot lose.
Each shard a part of who we are,
A truth beneath the distant star.

Through broken paths, we find our way,
In shadows cast by yesterday.
The remnants whisper, soft yet clear,
Awakening what we hold dear.

Together forged from shattered dreams,
A tapestry of silent themes.
In unity, we learn to stand,
Reclaimed by love, hand in hand.

So let us honor what has passed,
For in those pieces, we are cast.
Scattered remnants now entwined,
A testament to hearts aligned.

The Light Beneath the Charcoal

In the darkness, embers glow,
Hidden truths begin to show.
Beneath the soot and ash we find,
The spark of dreams left far behind.

Through the charcoal, a tale unfolds,
Of battles fought and courage bold.
Each layer thick, yet underneath,
A flicker breathes, a quiet heath.

With patience, we fan the flame,
Igniting hearts, no longer tame.
For beauty lies in the unseen,
A vibrant dance, a secret sheen.

So let us dig through years of grey,
To find the light that leads the way.
From ashes, hope begins to rise,
A testament beneath the skies.

In every heart, the charcoal fades,
Revealing light that never trades.
For in the depths of shadows cast,
The spirit's glow will ever last.

Song of the Searing Winds

Across the plains, the wild winds blow,
Carrying stories of ebb and flow.
A symphony of nature's might,
In every gust, the pulse ignites.

With every note, a whisper shared,
The dance of life, unprepared.
As branches sway and grasses bend,
The song continues, without end.

From mountain tops to valleys low,
The searing winds, a steady flow.
They weave through time, a timeless tale,
An echo haunting, sharp and pale.

Each breath the winds intend to take,
Reminds us of the storms we make.
Yet in their roar, a gentle grace,
Beneath the chaos, we find our place.

So let us dance to nature's song,
For in its rhythm, we belong.
The winds may sear, but hearts will mend,
In unity, we find our friend.

Radiant Resilience

In the heart of the storm, we stand tall,
With every setback, we rise and call.
Luminous spirits, never to bow,
In the face of fate, we take our vow.

Through trials of fire, our strength we find,
A tapestry woven, our fates entwined.
Each bruise a lesson, each scar a badge,
In the dance of life, we boldly engage.

Hope flickers bright in the shadowed night,
With courage ablaze, we chase the light.
In whispers of doubt, we hold our ground,
In the depths of chaos, our peace is found.

Together we rise, like the sun at dawn,
With arms outstretched, we carry on.
In the embrace of kindness, we grow,
Planting the seeds of love as we sow.

Resilience is gold in the world's embrace,
A luminous glow in the darkest space.
With every heartbeat, we break the mold,
In the story of life, our truth unfolds.

Traces of Ghostly Heat

In the still of the night, echoes remain,
A whisper of warmth, a subtle pain.
Ghostly shadows dance in the fading light,
Memories flicker, elusive as flight.

The air shimmers softly, tales untold,
Stories of lovers, both young and old.
Caught in the heat of a lingering glance,
Ghosts of the past still weave their romance.

Each breath of the wind carries their sighs,
Drifting like smoke beneath starry skies.
Fleeting moments etched in our core,
For every goodbye, there's always one more.

Heat that once pulsed in the veins anew,
Leaves behind traces, like morning dew.
In the depths of heart's chambers, they dwell,
Tamers of time with a haunting spell.

Through echoes of laughter, through whispers of tears,
The ghostly heat lingers through all the years.
In shadows they linger, in silence they speak,
In the warmth of the night, it's solace we seek.

From Dust to Dazzle

In the cradle of earth, where dreams begin,
Whispers of magic dance on the skin.
From particles lost to a radiant glow,
Resilience blooms where soft rivers flow.

Molded by time in a shimmering haze,
Each step we take turns the dull into blaze.
From shadows of doubt to the brilliance of day,
In the heart of the night, we boldly sway.

With hands reaching high for the stars above,
Casting aside fears, embracing love.
From ashes to glory, the journey unfolds,
In the fire of passion, our story is told.

Each grain of sand holds a secret untamed,
From dust to dazzle, the wild is unframed.
With every sunrise, we lift our heads high,
Transforming the mundane, we learn how to fly.

In the dance of the cosmos, our essence takes flight,
From dust we are born, into the light.
With every heartbeat, the world we amaze,
In the tapestry woven, we shine and blaze.

Heatwave of Change

In the swell of the season, tides do turn,
From embers of silence, the heart will yearn.
The heat of the moment beckons us near,
In the spark of change, we hold no fear.

Life crackles bright like the sun's embrace,
Bringing forth visions in vibrant space.
The world shifts and sighs with a breath so bold,
In the realm of the new, we break the mold.

Every heartbeat syncs with the rhythm of change,
With paths intertwined, life's patterns rearrange.
In the fires of passion, we're forged anew,
With courage ignited, we face the blue.

Through storms and through shadows, we dance with
grace,
Embracing the shifts that time will trace.
With every soul's journey, we carve a way,
In the dance of existence, we choose to stay.

As the heatwave rises, we shed the old skin,
In the canvas of life, let the color begin.
With hearts wide open, the future we claim,
In the warmth of the moment, we'll never be the same.

Rising Glow

The sun awakes in hues so bright,
Chasing shadows, igniting light.
Morning whispers, soft and low,
A dance begins in rising glow.

Flowers bloom, their petals spread,
In vibrant colors, brightly fed.
The world ignites, a canvas new,
Painting hopes in every hue.

Birds take flight, their songs arise,
Carving notes across the skies.
A symphony of life unfolds,
As daybreak's promise gently holds.

Mountains stand in silent grace,
Embracing time, the changing face.
In stillness lies the heart's refrain,
A testament to joy and pain.

Tides of time sweep over sand,
Footprints fade, but dreams expand.
With every dawn, we grow, we learn,
In the rising glow, we yearn.

Embers of Renewal

In quiet nights, the embers glow,
A fire's breath, soft winds that blow.
Under stars, the world feels small,
As whispers rise, and shadows fall.

Memories dance in flickered light,
Rekindled dreams take lofty flight.
Potentials spark in darkest days,
A path revealed in subtle ways.

Old leaves fall, but roots run deep,
Awakening life from winter's sleep.
New shoots emerge, embrace the sun,
As seasons change, we're all as one.

In ashes lie the seeds of fate,
Each flicker holds a tale innate.
Through trials faced and battles fought,
The embers glow, new hopes are sought.

From dusk to dawn, we find our way,
In every end, a bright new day.
Through pain and loss, we're made anew,
As embers rise, we breathe anew.

Phoenix Dreams

From ash and flame, a vision stirs,
In shadows deep, a spirit purrs.
A phoenix rises, bold and free,
Transforming dreams from what we see.

Colors blend in fiery flight,
Embracing darkness, forging light.
With wings outstretched, it takes a chance,
Dancing boldly in life's dance.

Through trials faced and bridges crossed,
From every wound, we've gained, not lost.
In flames of passion, hearts ignite,
As dreams take shape in star-lit night.

Echoes thrum in ancient lore,
Of journeys past, of open doors.
Rising higher, the spirit beams,
We find ourselves in phoenix dreams.

So let the fire cleanse the pain,
In every loss, a chance to gain.
We rise anew, forever bold,
In soaring visions, dreams unfold.

Rebirth in Silence

In gentle hush, the world awakes,
A canvas blank, where nature shakes.
In silent moments, truth prevails,
As whispers weave through hidden trails.

The earth exhales with tranquil grace,
Embracing life in every space.
From quietude, our spirits soar,
In rebirth's glow, we seek for more.

Stars will twinkle in velvet skies,
Guiding hearts with ancient ties.
In stillness, dreams begin to form,
As hope ignites a glowing warm.

Cycles turn, the seasons blend,
In every start, there lies an end.
From the silence, we learn to grow,
In every heartbeat, life's soft flow.

With open hearts, we shed the past,
And step towards the future fast.
In quiet moments, truths align,
We find rebirth in silence, divine.

Resurrecting Light

In shadows deep where sorrows lie,
A flicker warms, a soft reply.
From ashes gray, a flame stands tall,
The dawn arrives, dispelling all.

With every pulse, a heartbeat sings,
Renewing dreams that daylight brings.
Like petals kissed by morning dew,
A rebirth blooms, in every hue.

The whispered winds, they cheer, they dance,
In trust we step, in hope, in chance.
Each stride ignites the path ahead,
Through walls of doubt, our spirits led.

The stars emerge, a guiding light,
In darkest hours, they shine so bright.
For every loss, a lesson learned,
In this journey, our hearts returned.

Hope from the Ruins

Among the stones of shattered dreams,
New growth emerges, hope redeems.
Through cracks of time, a flower blooms,
Defying shadows, dispelling glooms.

The echoes of despair may fade,
Yet from the dust, our strength is made.
With every step, we lift our gaze,
To brighter skies, through smoky haze.

The sun will rise on broken ground,
A testament to love profound.
In every heart, resilience thrums,
A symphony as courage hums.

Together we reclaim the light,
With open arms, we hold it tight.
From ruins rise, our spirits soar,
In unity, forevermore.

Cinders of Tomorrow

In embered dreams where visions fade,
Hope flickers gently, unafraid.
From ashes scattered, new paths weave,
In twilight's grasp, we still believe.

The heart, a forge of every spark,
Ignites the night, dispels the dark.
With whispered tales of days to come,
We dance atop the loss, to drum.

Each breath a promise, bold and bright,
In cinders warm, we chase the light.
Through trials faced, love finds its way,
In every dawn, we herald day.

The future calls, its arms spread wide,
In unity, we stand, abide.
Cinders fade but dreams will last,
In fleeting moments, shadows cast.

A Trail of Glimmering Stars

Beneath the canopy of night,
A tapestry of endless light.
With every twinkle, tales unfold,
Of dreams departed, new ones bold.

The moon whispers secrets old,
As silver beams in silence fold.
In every heart, a wish takes flight,
To wander wide through star-kissed night.

A journey marked by glimmer's grace,
Each step illuminated space.
Through shadows cast, we find our way,
In constellations, hope will stay.

Together there, beneath the skies,
We chase the stars with open eyes.
For every heartbeat, love will turn,
In this vast cosmos, brightly burn.

The Heart of Smoldering Remnants

In shadows deep where embers lie,
Silent whispers of time gone by.
Ashen dreams in the moon's glow,
A heart beats soft, yet doth not know.

The warmth that flickered fades away,
Memories linger, colors sway.
Charred remains of a fierce delight,
Awake now, the whispers of night.

From glowing coals, a story shared,
Of passion bright, and love declared.
Yet in the silence, shadows creep,
Wrapped in secrets, the soul must keep.

Time may cool the fiery dance,
Yet in the dark, there's still a chance.
To cherish embers, hold them close,
In aching hearts, they still can boast.

And when the dawn breaks new and bright,
The remnants glow with hopeful light.
For life anew will start to bloom,
In hearts reborn, dispelling gloom.

A Sonnet for the Scattered Ash

Oh, scattered ash upon the breeze,
Once fierce flames that roared with ease.
A gentle sigh, a soft goodnight,
In quiet corners, lost from sight.

Each particle, a story told,
In whispered tales of brave and bold.
The warmth once shared, the dreams now gone,
Yet in the dusk, our spirits dawn.

Amidst the dust, a hint of grace,
In every trace, there's love's embrace.
Though time has passed and changed the scene,
The echoes linger, soft and keen.

So raise a toast to what once burned,
To fleeting passions and lessons learned.
In scattered ash, the love remains,
In silent shadows, the heart retains.

From every fragment, let there rise,
A memory that never dies.
For as the embers fade away,
Their light still dances in the sway.

Breathing Life into Coal

In darkened depths where silence reigns,
A flicker stirs within the chains.
Coal lies waiting, cold and still,
Yet life courses with a will.

With every breath, the tension builds,
In hidden depths, a spirit yields.
From hidden heart, the warmth will spread,
Through layers thick, where dreams are bred.

Bring forth the spark, the flame to rise,
In glowing warmth, the truth belies.
Every heartbeat, every sigh,
Will breathe the fire that won't comply.

From coal to flame, the journey vast,
Rebirth ignites, the die is cast.
With open heart, come gather round,
For in the fire, our souls are found.

So take this moment, hold it tight,
As coal ignites into the night.
In this embrace of heat and soul,
Together we will make us whole.

After the Burn

After the burn, what remains?
A scar of love, through joy and pain.
The ashes settle, stories fade,
Yet in the stillness, dreams parade.

The wounds once raw, now softly heal,
In quiet moments, we can feel.
From fire's end, a lesson learned,
In hearts, the hopeful ember burned.

We gather strength from what has passed,
In memories that hold us fast.
Through every tear, we find our way,
In light that comes, a brand new day.

So let us rise, like Phoenix bird,
From the debris, let love be stirred.
For after burn, there's space to grow,
In whispered winds, our spirits flow.

With every heartbeat, let us strive,
To carry forth, to truly thrive.
In ashes soft, our path is laid,
In life reborn, no dreams delayed.

Whispers of Forgotten Flames

In shadows cast by time's embrace,
Old embers hum a soft, lost tune.
They speak of warmth in empty space,
Of flickering hearts beneath the moon.

Each whisper tells of a glowing past,
Of stories wrapped in whispers' thread.
Yet every flame, no matter how vast,
Must one day lay to rest its head.

Forgotten sparks lie deep within,
In corners dark where dreams reside.
But every end, where loss begins,
Can light the path to what's inside.

With gentle winds, the flames revive,
A dance of hope, a brush with fate.
For in the depths, we learn to strive,
And turn the loss to something great.

So hear the whispers, feel the heat,
Of flames that teach us to embrace.
In every loss, there's life complete,
A chance to find a brighter place.

Reignited Spirits

In the quiet, a spark will rise,
From ashes soft, a fire anew.
Dreams awaken, casting sighs,
Inviting passions to break through.

With every breath, the air ignites,
A dance of shadows, light, and grace.
The heart beats strong, it knows its rights,
In trials faced, we find our place.

Rekindled souls, we chase the dawn,
With hands held high, we claim the light.
The chains of doubt are overdrawn,
As spirits soar, prepared for flight.

We rise like phoenix from the grey,
With laughter bright, we'll face the fight.
Each step we take will pave the way,
For paths unseen, our hearts alight.

In unity, our strength combines,
With every heartbeat, hope will gleam.
Together we will break the binds,
Reignited spirits, living dream.

The Glow Beyond the Grit

Beneath the struggles, hope remains,
A quiet glow that softly shines.
Through every storm, through all the pains,
It whispers faith in fragile lines.

When shadows fall and darkness sways,
The grit we bear becomes our guide.
In every challenge, light displays,
A strength within we cannot hide.

The fire of dreams, though dimmed a bit,
Can spark to life with just a thought.
In every heart, there lies a wit,
Where courage rises, battles fought.

With every step on tangled roads,
We weave our stories into light.
The glow beyond the grit explodes,
A tapestry of love and fight.

So cherish scars, they tell our tale,
Of triumph found in lessons learned.
For in the struggle, we unveil,
The glow that through the grit has burned.

Ashen Paths to Tomorrow

Upon the ashes, paths unfold,
Where dreams once danced and colors gleamed.
In silent moments, futures told,
Of hopes reborn, and souls redeemed.

The echoes of the past persist,
As whispers wane in twilight's gleam.
Each step we take, we must insist,
On carving light from every dream.

Through ashen trails, we learn to tread,
With hearts that brave the weathered road.
In every tear and word unsaid,
We gather strength, we share the load.

For every end is just a gate,
To new beginnings, fresh and bright.
In every heart, we cultivate,
The sparks that lead us to the light.

So let us walk with heads held high,
On ashen paths that shape our way.
For through the dark, we find the sky,
And greet the dawn of a new day.

Ashen Wings

In twilight's glow, where shadows creep,
Ashen wings take flight, secrets to keep.
Whispers of loss in the silent air,
Echoes of dreams hang heavy with care.

Dusty trails lead to forgotten lands,
Where memory clings like fine grains of sand.
The weight of silence, a lingering ghost,
In the quiet dusk, we search for the lost.

Beneath the skies of a fading realm,
A flicker of hope at the helm.
With each beat, the shadows entwine,
Yet in the darkness, a spark can shine.

Through night's embrace, we learn to soar,
With ashen wings, we'll seek evermore.
In the depths of sorrow, we find our way,
Through the scattered embers of yesterday.

Together we rise, on the winds of fate,
With ashen wings, we embrace our state.
For every fallen dream must mend,
In the ashes, new beginnings blend.

Tides of Transformation

The ocean stirs with a restless sigh,
Tides of change whisper and fly.
Waves crash hard on the barren shore,
Each swell, each fall, opens a door.

In the silver moonlight, hearts awaken,
The power of water, a force unshaken.
With every ebb, old fears subside,
In the shifting sands, we find our tide.

Beneath the surface, life reclaims,
Colors and shapes, both wild and tame.
Nature's embrace, a vibrant call,
In the dance of tides, we rise and fall.

As dawn breaks forth with a golden hue,
Promising paths both old and new.
Embrace the currents, let go of the past,
Ride the waves of change, fierce and fast.

For transformation flows like the sea,
A beautiful journey, setting us free.
In the tides of life, we find our song,
With every rhythm, we know we belong.

A New Dawn's Promise

As the night yields to morning's grace,
A new dawn rises, a warm embrace.
Golden rays spill over the hills,
Whispers of hope, the heart gently thrills.

In the tapestry woven with threads of light,
Dreams take flight, banishing night.
With each sunrise, our spirits renew,
The promise of paths yet to view.

Soft petals open in the gentle breeze,
Nature awakens, playful with ease.
The world ignites with colors so bright,
Each moment alive, a pure delight.

With every heartbeat, the future unfolds,
New stories written, adventures bold.
In the dawn's tender glow, we find our way,
Chasing the shadows that dared to play.

Together we rise, hand in hand,
Rejoicing in life, our hearts expand.
A new dawn waits, let us not fear,
For every new day, the path is clear.

Beneath the Charred Surface

Amidst the ashes of long-lost flames,
Beneath the surface, new life claims.
Charred remnants whisper tales of the past,
Within the darkness, shadows are cast.

Yet in the soil, the roots will grow,
Transforming pain into a radiant glow.
Out of the ruins, strength will arise,
Where hope once flickered, a fire flies.

Each scar tells stories, each crack a sign,
Resilience blooms in a design so fine.
Beneath the charred, a vibrant heart beats,
A testament of life, in defeat it greets.

With soft tendrils reaching for the light,
The journey of healing, a courageous flight.
From ashes to blossoms, the cycle spins,
Where endings dwell, a new life begins.

So let us honor the journeys we take,
The beauty in darkness, the strength in the ache.
Beneath the surface, great wonders reside,
In the heart of destruction, new worlds abide.

Smokescreen of Possibility

In the haze, dreams flutter and weave,
Possibilities hide, yet still believe.
Whispers dance through the murky air,
A tapestry born from hope and dare.

Shadows twist, revealing the light,
Each spark ignites in the depths of night.
Paths unfold, a labyrinth of grace,
Beyond the veil, there's a waiting place.

In the chaos, clarity awaits,
Every breath exudes what fate creates.
With each inhale, visions expand,
An open heart, a brave new land.

The smokescreen shimmers, a portal vast,
Through time and space, we journey fast.
With tenacity, we chase the fire,
In the unknown, we find desire.

Hope rises, as dawn begins to break,
A world anew, for our own sake.
In the embers, potential thrums,
Beyond the smokescreen, possibility hums.

Castles of Char

In ashes strewn, foundations lie,
Once mighty homes, now a quiet sigh.
Battlements high, they dream no more,
Cinders whisper tales of yore.

Echoes linger, in shadows cast,
Memories linger, from shadows past.
With every crack, a story told,
In these ruins, hearts grow bold.

Though char remains, the spirit's strong,
From fiery depths, we rebuild the song.
Each brick of loss, a step we tread,
In castles of char, new dreams are bred.

Together we stand, amidst the brume,
In the heart of loss, we find our bloom.
Through every scar, resilience grows,
In castles of char, the future glows.

We gather the strength from the earth below,
With fire's embrace, our intentions flow.
From the remnants, we forge our way,
In castles of char, we rise each day.

Unfurling from the Scorch

From bitter burns, new life awakes,
Tender shoots push through the flakes.
In the heat, resilience finds,
A beauty hidden in fragile minds

With each embrace of the blazing sun,
Nature's promise has just begun.
Leaves unfurl with a gentle grace,
Emerging life in a scorched-space.

The air is thick with fragrant dreams,
Blossoms bloom near bubbling streams.
Hope emerges where fire laid waste,
In the scorching light, we find our haste.

Roots entwine in the earth's warm hold,
Drawing strength from everything bold.
In the aftermath, a vibrant rush,
Unfurling from the scorch, life starts to blush.

Seasons turn, and still we thrive,
In the remnants of flames, we come alive.
Amongst the ashes, beauty soars high,
Unfurling from the scorch, beneath the sky.

The Light Beneath the Ashes

In the quiet hush of the morning mist,
Where dreams converge and hope persists.
Beneath the remnants, hearts ignite,
A flicker glows in the dark of night.

Whispers of warmth beneath the cold,
Stories of courage, quietly told.
In every shadow, a spark they find,
The light beneath, forever kind.

With patience, the embers softly warm,
In the fiercest storm, we find our form.
Through every trial, we'll stand our ground,
The light beneath, forever bound.

From the ashes, we rise and shine,
In every heart, the light divine.
Through the struggles, love prevails,
In shimmering beams, our spirit sails.

Never lost, in the darkest hour,
Hope will bloom like a vibrant flower.
With faith in what the heart can see,
The light beneath the ashes sets us free.

From Ceaseless Flicker

In shadows cast by whispering light,
A dance unfolds, bold yet slight,
Flickers call, in the quiet night,
Echoes of dreams, taking flight.

The silence hums, a gentle breeze,
Cradling hopes like autumn leaves,
With every heartbeat, it weaves,
Stories of love, that never leave.

Time slips through a golden sieve,
Moments cherished, before we grieve,
In ceaseless flicker, we believe,
A spark remains, we shall cleave.

Light reveals what dusk conceals,
Unfurling truth, as it reveals,
Life's tapestry with vibrant reels,
From flicker born, each heart heals.

And as the dawn begins to rise,
Hope takes flight in painted skies,
From ceaseless flicker, never dies,
Our spirits soar, where love complies.

Remnants of Radiance

In twilight's grasp where shadows blend,
Remnants speak of journeys penned,
Echoes linger, time won't mend,
Threads of memories, softly send.

Fading sunlight, golden hue,
Whispers of the past, ring true,
In gentle sighs, the heart renews,
Each moment lived, a vivid view.

Stars emerge in cascading grace,
Lighting paths that time can trace,
In quiet night, we find our place,
Remnants of radiance, we embrace.

With every heartbeat, stories bind,
In every soul, a world confined,
In echoes soft, we're intertwined,
The glow remains, not left behind.

When dawn awakens, shadows fade,
But remnants hold the love we've made,
Through every trial, we are laid,
In radiant bonds, forever stayed.

Foundations of Fire

Beneath the embers, whispers grow,
Foundations laid, where passions flow,
Through fiery hearts, the truth we sow,
In every glow, our spirits know.

The flames that dance, time can't erase,
Illuminating dreams we chase,
Through darkest nights, we find our grace,
In the warmth of love's embrace.

Chaos brews in the wildest storm,
Yet in our souls, a spark is born,
From ashes rise, the new and worn,
Foundations strong, with hope adorned.

We gather strength, in unity bright,
Our voices merge, a shared delight,
Together, we ignite the night,
In this fierce blaze, we take flight.

With every flame, a story told,
Of dreams ignited, fierce and bold,
Foundations of fire, never cold,
In hearts ablaze, our love unfolds.

The Breath of Renewal

In quiet dawn, the world awakes,
With gentle sighs, the moment breaks,
Each breath we take, the earth remakes,
In whispers soft, a heart unshakes.

The morning dew, like crystal tears,
Refreshes hopes and calms our fears,
In every beat, the past disappears,
The breath of renewal, time adheres.

Nature's grace, a sacred flow,
In fragrant blooms, new life will grow,
Each petal kissed by sun's warm glow,
The circle spins, as seasons know.

From ashes rise the dreams reborn,
We shed the weight, embrace the morn,
In every sigh, a new adorn,
The breath of renewal, hope is sworn.

So let us walk, hand in hand anew,
In every step, the earth's bright hue,
Together crafting skies of blue,
With every breath, our spirits grew.

Echoes in the Ember

In the darkness, whispers play,
Ghostly shadows dance and sway.
Memories flicker in the night,
Embers glow with ancient light.

Voices linger, soft and low,
Tales of love that ebb and flow.
Brighter sparks in quiet hearts,
From the past, the flame imparts.

Time stands still in quiet grace,
Echoes find their rightful place.
Through the years, they gently weave,
Stories told that we believe.

Each flicker holds a soul's desire,
Fueling dreams with whispered fire.
In the twilight, we take flight,
Chasing visions in the night.

As the dawn begins to break,
Embers fade, but hearts won't shake.
With hope's light, we start anew,
In the warmth, our dreams shine true.

The Unfolding of a Dream

In the silence, dreams take shape,
Wings of thought begin to scrape.
Ideas bloom, like flowers rare,
Whispers of what we might dare.

Through the haze, a vision clear,
Guiding us through doubt and fear.
Fingers trace the path we seek,
Every heartbeat, strong and meek.

With each sunrise, colors blend,
Promises we weave and mend.
In the canvas of the day,
Shadows blend and drift away.

Over mountains, under stars,
We bear witness to our scars.
From the ashes, hope will gleam,
As we chase the fragile dream.

In the twilight, truths emerge,
Guiding hearts with gentle surge.
In this dance, we find our song,
Together, where we all belong.

Songs of the Searing Soil

In the fields where the wild crops grow,
Stories sung with every blow.
Roots entwined in earth so deep,
Promises of harvest keep.

Beneath the sun's relentless gaze,
Sweat and toil in endless praise.
Echoes of what life can yield,
Nurtured dreams in fertile field.

When the storm clouds darkly loom,
Nature's grace can bring the bloom.
From the tempest, life will rise,
Songs of strength that never dies.

Harmony in every grain,
Lessons learned through joy and pain.
As we labor, hands in soil,
In our hearts, the song of toil.

Together we will sow our fate,
Opening arms to cultivate.
With each season, we embrace,
The dance of life, our sacred space.

Shades of the Fallen Flame

When the fire dims to shades of gray,
Bitter winds begin to play.
Whispers linger in the dusk,
Echoes fading into husk.

Flickers of a once-bright glow,
Remnants of the heat we know.
In the ashes, spirits rise,
Building dreams that never die.

With each heartbeat, silence grows,
Pulsing softly, ebbing flows.
In the quiet, stories dwell,
Fading tales of heaven and hell.

Embers carry what's been lost,
Finding warmth despite the cost.
From the darkness, light will break,
In the stillness, hearts awake.

Through the night, we navigate,
Finding solace, learning fate.
Every shade a lesson learned,
In the flame, our spirits burned.

As dawn arrives with golden hue,
We hold on to what rings true.
In the shadows, love remains,
Guiding us through life's refrains.

Wings of the Firebird

In twilight skies, a tale takes flight,
A firebird glows, with wings of light.
Through the shadows, it brightly soars,
Bringing warmth to forgotten shores.

With every beat, the embers dance,
A rhythm of hope, a second chance.
It whispers secrets, ancient and bold,
Of dreams reborn, of stories told.

In flames of gold, it finds its way,
Through darkened nights and brighter days.
Each flicker sparkles, a guiding star,
Leading lost souls, no matter how far.

The freedom song within its roar,
Echoing life and so much more.
With hues of passion, it paints the sky,
As hearts awaken, learning to fly.

From ashes rise, a new dawn breaks,
With each flight, the earth remakes.
The wings that burn, now blessing the night,
As the firebird claims its rightful flight.

Secrets within the Smoke

In swirling haze, the whispers blend,
A tale obscured, where shadows bend.
Each curling wisp, a story tight,
Of dreams and fears, woven in light.

The secrets spun from ashes past,
Are cloaked in mystery, holding fast.
To breathe the smoke is to know the fire,
Of hearts that ache and souls that aspire.

With every puff, a vision glows,
Of paths untaken, of winter snows.
Embers buried beneath the gray,
Reveal the treasures of yesterday.

Yet hidden truth waits to ignite,
In shadows deep, it yearns for light.
Each fragrant tendril curiously calls,
Unveiling the strength that within us sprawls.

So hold your breath; let the smoke entice,
For every secret comes with a price.
In searching the haze, we come to find,
The beauty and chaos of heart and mind.

Transformation of the Charcoal Soul

Beneath the gray, the blackened heart,
A charcoal soul awaits its part.
In stillness, passion sleeps in deep,
While echoes of dreams begin to creep.

From ashes cold, a spark ignites,
Turning shadows into vibrant sights.
The canvas dark, yet rich with lore,
Becomes a tapestry to explore.

In gentle flames, the embers rise,
A metamorphosis, a bold surprise.
The charcoal crumbles, dust in air,
Rebirth through fire—beyond despair.

With every flicker, strength unfolds,
A testimony of shadows bold.
Transformation sings, a radiant call,
Emerging light, dispelling the fall.

The alchemy of time and grace,
Turns charcoal's weight to a warm embrace.
So trust the fire, let your spirit soar,
For within the ash, lies so much more.

Ashen Past, Bright Future

In quiet corners, memories dwell,
An ashen past, time's subtle spell.
Like dust that settles on a page,
Echoes of laughter, joy, and rage.

But time moves on, like rivers flow,
Each moment whispered, every sorrow.
From charred remains, a seed takes root,
A promise of life, a brand new shoot.

With every dawn, the sun will rise,
Chasing shadows, painting the skies.
What once was lost, now finds its voice,
In harmony, we learn to rejoice.

The ashen past, a fertile ground,
Where lessons learned are tightly bound.
In every scar, a story lives,
Of all that's taken, all that it gives.

So let the future call your name,
With open arms, embrace the flame.
For ashes tell of all we've been,
And bright tomorrows await within.

The Beauty of Regrowth

Beneath the frost, new life does stir,
Hope emerges, a gentle blur.
From ashes rise the silent seeds,
Nature whispers, fulfill her needs.

Soft green shoots through soil break free,
Kissing sun, they dance with glee.
A canvas fresh, a vibrant hue,
Reminds us all of what is true.

With every storm, we learn to bend,
Through all the loss, we find a friend.
The cycle turns, we embrace the pain,
For beauty comes when we remain.

A withered branch, now bearing leaves,
Speaks of strength, the heart believes.
In nature's grasp, we find our way,
The beauty blooms, day by day.

Regrowth teaches, with tender care,
That after night, light will declare.
A promise kept, a silent vow,
In every bud, we learn to bow.

Smoke Signals of Change

In twilight's hush, the embers glow,
A whisper stirs, the soft winds blow.
Messages rise, with secrets untold,
In smoky trails, the futures unfold.

From dusk till dawn, the shadows weave,
In twilight's grip, we dare believe.
A flicker here, a spark gone wild,
Signals of change, enchanting and mild.

The sky absorbs each shifting tone,
Like dreams half-baked, yet bravely sown.
New paths await in every whiff,
As the world breathes in, each hopeful gift.

With every curl, a story's cast,
The present fades, shaped by the past.
Smoke may linger, then softly part,
But traces remain, igniting the heart.

Let go the fears, let worries cease,
In this moment, embrace your peace.
Change beckons near, like a dancer's call,
With smoke signals bright, we rise or fall.

Brighter than Before

In shadows deep, a light does gleam,
A spark of hope, a waking dream.
From darkest nights, the dawn appears,
A promise made to calm our fears.

With every step, we rise anew,
The skies above take on a blue.
The warmth of sun, a gentle embrace,
Guiding us forth to a brighter space.

In every heart, a fire burns bright,
Chasing away the lingering night.
With open arms, we greet the day,
And leave behind the past's dismay.

Brighter than before, we take our stance,
In life's grand rhythm, we learn to dance.
For every scar, a story told,
A tapestry woven, rich and bold.

Through trials faced, we grow wise,
Reflecting strength in our own eyes.
Together we shine, in love we trust,
Resilient souls, from dust to dust.

Bereft Yet Blooming

In silence deep, my heart does ache,
Yet from the cracks, new blooms awake.
A paradox of joy and pain,
In this embrace, I learn to gain.

Petals soft, on barren ground,
Speak of love that's lost, yet found.
Through sorrow's grip, the colors rise,
Against the odds, they reach the skies.

With every tear, a seed is sown,
In every loss, a truth is grown.
From depths of grief, a beauty's born,
A strength to carry us each morn.

The world can break, yet still we stand,
In fragile blooms, we find our hand.
Each moment shared, a heartbeat's call,
In bereft fields, we rise for all.

Though darkness lingers, we find our way,
With flowers bright, we greet the day.
For in this journey, we learn to see,
That even in loss, we can be free.

Resilient Roots

In the soil where shadows lie,
Seeds of strength begin to grow.
Beneath the weight of all that's nigh,
They reach for light, and stretch, and show.

Whispers of winds, they bend and sway,
Tales of storms that tried to break.
Yet they stand firm, come what may,
Their spirit strong, they never shake.

Through the frost and fleeting time,
They gather warmth within their core.
Silent strength in whispered rhyme,
Roots entwined, forever more.

With every trial, they grow robust,
Nurtured by the earth's embrace.
In hardship, they find their trust,
A testament to life's vast grace.

Emerging from the darkened depths,
Resilient roots, they claim their place.
In the dance of life, their steps,
Are etched in nature's sacred space.

Glimmering among Gray

In the mist where shadows tread,
A flicker lights the weary air.
Amidst the dull, and often dread,
Hope's reflection glimmers there.

A spark ignites the heart's lost dream,
Against the cliffs of despair's steep climb.
With every breath, it starts to beam,
Radiating warmth, through space and time.

Through stormy skies, it finds a way,
To pierce the cloud with vibrant hue.
In frozen moments, it will stay,
A beacon bright, forever true.

As darkened days weave threads of night,
This little light, it holds its ground.
For in its glow, we find the sight,
Of brighter paths, with joy unbound.

Though shadows loom, they cannot hide,
The spark that keeps the spirit flying.
In hearts of many, it won't subside,
A gentle glow, forever trying.

Reawakening the Undying

In the quiet of the stillness,
Where whispers of the ages sigh,
Life's pulse beats with thrilling thrillness,
Awakening dreams that never die.

From ashes cold, new fires rise,
Filling the void with vibrant cheer.
Amidst the ruins, hope defies,
Relighting paths once lost in fear.

Colors spill where gray was found,
Nature weaving threads of fate.
Through broken ground, life's song resounds,
Rebirth ignites, it's never late.

In every tear, a longing stirs,
A chance to grow, to reach anew.
Through every heart, the spirit purrs,
Embracing light, and all that's true.

So rise from depths where shadows creep,
Embrace the dawn, the time ascends.
In every soul, a promise deep,
Reawakening, where love transcends.

Beneath the Veil of Soot

Under layers, thick and dark,
Lies a world of hidden grace.
Beneath despair's heavy mark,
Hope's sweet whispers leave a trace.

Through the grime, a light once shone,
Guiding hands through empty night.
In silence, seeds of strength are sown,
Flickering waits, to spark the bright.

Threads of gold won't fade away,
Though obscured by the tumult's shroud.
With each dawn, they fight the gray,
Emerging fierce, they make us proud.

As soot may cling and time may wear,
Beneath it all, a fire burns.
A strength that lifts, a will to care,
In every heart, the world returns.

So cast away the veil of gloom,
Discover what lies deep within.
There blooms a life that dares to bloom,
A tapestry where hope begins.

Echoes of the Past

Footsteps linger on the ground,
Memories whisper all around.
Shadows dance in fading light,
Stories woven through the night.

Silent echoes softly call,
In the stillness, they enthrall.
Time marches on, yet we stand,
With the past held in our hands.

Faded photos, worn and torn,
From the ashes, new can be born.
History tells us where we've been,
In every joy, in every sin.

Voices of the long-gone years,
Carried forward through our tears.
Lessons learned and battles fought,
In the silence, solace sought.

As we tread on ancient ground,
In the echoes, hope is found.
Through the maze of time we roam,
In these echoes, we find home.

Flames that Forge

In the heart where fire burns,
Each flame awaits, the lesson learns.
From the heat, we find our way,
Strength is built in trials we face.

Embers spark in darkest night,
Guiding dreams towards the light.
Molding courage with each blaze,
Shaping paths through life's maze.

Fires dance, they twist and turn,
In their glow, our spirits yearn.
For the heat can heal and scar,
Transforming us to who we are.

Through the flames, we rise anew,
With a heart that's bold and true.
Each flicker tells a vibrant tale,
Of hearts ablaze that will not pale.

So let the sparks ignite the night,
For in the struggle, we find light.
With every flame, our spirits thrive,
In the forge, we learn to live.

Whispers of the Resilient

In the quiet, strength resides,
Hope and courage are our guides.
Through the storms that shake our roots,
Tiny whispers spark our truths.

As the winds begin to wane,
Voices rise above the pain.
From the ashes, flowers bloom,
Resilient hearts dispel the gloom.

Every tear that hits the ground,
Fuels the spirit, love unbound.
In the struggle, we take flight,
Together facing darkest night.

Though the road is rough and long,
Together, we will find our song.
With each step, we stand so tall,
In unity, we conquer all.

Whispers weave through every trial,
In the silence, find our smile.
Those who stumble find their way,
In the whispers of each day.

Phoenix in Flight

From the flames, a creature soars,
Wings unfurl, the spirit roars.
Rising high, through ash and smoke,
With each beat, the past is broke.

A symbol of renewal bright,
In the darkness, brings the light.
Through the trials, pain and strife,
Emerges bold, embracing life.

Colors flash against the sky,
Painting dreams that never die.
With each cycle, strength is gained,
In the journey, hope unchained.

Soaring through the open air,
Leaving behind the weight of care.
Trust the fire, trust the flight,
As we chase the wings of light.

In the heart where embers glow,
Life's a dance, a bold tableau.
From the ashes, we ignite,
Like the phoenix, we take flight.

New Roots in Old Soil

In shadows deep, old whispers grow,
New roots break forth, seeking the glow.
From earth's embrace, they strive and yearn,
For sunlight's kiss, their fate to learn.

Beneath the weight of stories told,
A quiet strength begins to unfold.
A tapestry rich, of past and now,
In every twist, they find their vow.

Rustling leaves, a gentle sigh,
The ancient ground, where dreams can fly.
With patience stitched into each seam,
They weave a future, thread by dream.

Through stormy nights, and morning dew,
They stretch and reach, as if they knew.
Old soil cradles hope anew,
In every shift, the life renews.

Thus, roots entwined, they softly dance,
In rhythm with fate, they take their chance.
From past to present, they intertwine,
In whispers low, their hearts align.

The Warmth of Restart

A piano's note, a gentle beam,
Life hums anew, awakening dream.
With open hearts, we rise from fall,
Embrace the dawn, hear the call.

As ashes fade, a spark ignites,
Each moment shines, with new delights.
In mirror's gaze, we shed the past,
Unfolding truth, as shadows cast.

Waves crash softly, lessons learned,
In the ebb, we feel our yearn.
Each stumble turns to dance with grace,
In every step, we find our place.

With steady hands, we beat the drum,
To rhythms bright, we overcome.
Life's canvas waits, so vast and wide,
In strokes of hope, we choose our stride.

So take a breath, let courage swell,
In now's embrace, we weave the spell.
With every heartbeat, we restart,
The warmth of life ignites the heart.

Unfurling from the Blackened

From ashes thick, a whisper stirs,
A tender shoot, through darkness blurs.
It reaches high, defies the night,
Emerging bold, into the light.

Each fragile leaf, a tale begun,
Of battles fought, of hope re-spun.
Through cracks of earth, they brave the fight,
Transforming pain to pure delight.

With every breath, resistance fades,
As new horizons craft their shades.
In vibrant hues, the colors blend,
A tapestry that will not end.

The past, a shadow, lingers still,
Yet roots grow deeper, shape their will.
For every storm that bends and breaks,
A stronger voice, the silence shakes.

So let them rise, from blackened ground,
In beauty found, new strength is crowned.
With every unfurl, they reclaim their song,
In nature's arms, where they belong.

Blaze of the Aspiring

A flicker found in depths unseen,
The spark ignites, a vibrant sheen.
With force of will, they twist and turn,
In every heart, a fire burns.

Beyond the clouds, where dreams take flight,
They reach for stars, embrace the night.
With whispers bold, they catch the flame,
In every heart, they learn their name.

Through trials faced, they build their core,
With every step, they seek for more.
Pushing boundaries, they'll not relent,
In joy and pain, they find content.

A blaze of passion, fierce and bright,
Illuminates the darkest night.
With hands held high, they pave the way,
With every dream, they seize the day.

So let them soar, the aspiring souls,
In every story, a place that holds.
For flames that dance, they mark the trail,
In blazing hearts, they shall not fail.

Phoenix's Flight

From ashes risen, bold and bright,
A spirit soaring, taking flight.
With wings of fire, it leaves the ground,
In vibrant colors, hope is found.

Through skies of dusk, it glides and sways,
Embracing warmth of golden rays.
In every shimmer, stories told,
Of courage lived, of heart so bold.

It dances on the winds of time,
In whispered winds, a subtle rhyme.
A symbol fierce, of life's return,
In every heart, its flames still burn.

The journey bright, the past behind,
A vibrant world, a path defined.
Through storms it flies, relentless, free,
The essence of eternity.

So follow its flight, embrace the fire,
In every fall, find sweet desire.
For like the phoenix, rise anew,
A heartbeat strong, a dream come true.

Silent Resurgence

In shadows deep, where whispers dwell,
A quiet strength begins to swell.
From silent springs, life starts to bloom,
In hushed moments, dispelling gloom.

The earth awakens, breathes anew,
With hidden hopes and skies so blue.
Each bud unfurls, a tale unfolds,
Of resilience in the cold.

With a gentle touch, the bloom appears,
Erasing doubt, softening fears.
In stillness found, a vibrant spark,
A flame ignites, igniting dark.

The past recedes, in whispers lost,
Each heartbeat gains, no matter the cost.
For in the silence, power grows,
A symphony that softly flows.

Embrace the calm, the change it brings,
For in the quiet, life still sings.
Through every breath, rise and believe,
In silent strength, we learn to weave.

Charred Dreams

In the shadows where dreams were laid,
Charred remains of hopes displayed.
Once bright visions, now turned to dust,
Yet from the ashes, we learn to trust.

Through twisted paths, the heart still seeks,
In broken words, the spirit speaks.
Each ember glows, a story told,
Of battles fought, of dreams turned bold.

The scars remind us of the past,
Yet hold the strength to rise at last.
With every crack, a light will find,
The beauty strong, the heart refined.

So linger not in sorrow's hold,
For from the fire, we'll be consoled.
With charred dreams, we find our way,
To brighter skies, to a new day.

Embrace the pain, let it ignite,
A fierce resolve to stand and fight.
Each charred dream, a lesson learned,
In every heart, a fire burns.

New Beginnings

A dawn breaks soft, with whispers light,
As shadows flee and take to flight.
In every heartbeat, life reclaimed,
For with each sunrise, we're unchained.

The canvas waits, for colors bright,
To paint the dreams we've held so tight.
With brush in hand, we start anew,
Each stroke a promise, bold and true.

The road ahead, with twists and turns,
Through every challenge, passion burns.
For every step, a lesson sown,
In fields of hope, we all have grown.

Let fears dissolve like mist at dawn,
In every ending, a new song drawn.
So let the past breathe its farewell,
As new beginnings start to swell.

With open hearts, embrace the ride,
For in our journeys, love will guide.
Through every chapter, let it sing,
A tale of life, of new beginnings.

Flames of Tomorrow

The stars above in silence glow,
While dreams take flight in night's soft flow.
With hearts ablaze, we chase the light,
Guided by flames of pure delight.

In every flicker, visions rise,
A tapestry of endless skies.
For what we seek, it waits in fire,
Igniting hope, inspiring desire.

Through trials faced, and tears that fell,
The flames of tomorrow weave a spell.
With courage forged in every day,
We'll find the strength to light the way.

So chase the night, embrace the spark,
In every shadow, leave a mark.
For in the dance of flame and dream,
Tomorrow's light will always gleam.

With every dawn, the fire glows,
A promise shared, as the heart knows.
In flames of tomorrow, we shall rise,
A symphony sung across the skies.

Glows in the Gloom

In whispers soft, the night descends,
Where shadows weave, and silence bends.
A flicker found in darkest place,
With glowing light, a warm embrace.

Through tangled roots and misty air,
Hope lingers still, a glimmer rare.
Each star a guide, a spark, a dream,
Illuminating the gentle stream.

The moonlight dances on the floor,
With silver touch, it seeks the door.
It calls the heart to find its song,
In glows of night, where we belong.

As shadows stretch and time proceeds,
With every pulse, the night still feeds.
A lantern held by hands unseen,
A glow that whispers all serene.

The Dance of the Departed

In twilight's haze, they take their flight,
The souls that weave through velvet night.
With every step, the echoes play,
In silence lost, they find their way.

A gentle breeze, a brush of skin,
In shadows deep, their voices spin.
Their laughter lingers, a haunting sound,
As memories lost are finally found.

Through ancient woods where secrets sigh,
The dance of dreams will never die.
In every rustle, a tale unfolds,
Of love and loss, of hearts so bold.

They twist and turn, a spectral waltz,
In moonlight's glow, we share their pulse.
With every twirl, a story shared,
In the dance of life, they are declared.

Shadows of the Spent Fuel

In darkened corners, shadows blend,
Remnants of fire where embers end.
A flicker dims, a story told,
Of warmth consumed, of dreams gone cold.

The whispers haunt the quiet space,
Ghosts of brilliance in empty grace.
Each shadow holds a past affair,
Moments captured, beyond compare.

Yet from the ashes, time will sprout,
A flicker reignites, dispels the doubt.
For what was lost can rise anew,
In shadows cast, the potential grew.

A dance of light in corners found,
Reflects the journey, the strength unbound.
Fueling tomorrow's bright ascent,
From shadows deep, their stories meant.

From Grime to Shine

In alleyways where lost dreams roam,
There lies a place that calls to home.
Through grime and grit, the heart will beat,
With every step, it finds its feet.

The sun will rise, the dust will clear,
In every struggle, hope draws near.
A canvas blank, a chance to bloom,
From darkened paths, we chase the loom.

With every bruise, a tale to tell,
Transcending pain, we break the shell.
In laughter's glow, the spirit twines,
From broken shards, the beauty shines.

So let the journey mark the day,
Through trials faced, we find our way.
In every crack, the light defines,
From grime to shine, the heart aligns.

The Rekindling Flame

In the shadows where memories play,
Whispers of warmth begin to sway.
Hearts once cold start to ignite,
As hope returns with soft twilight.

Flickers dance in the night's embrace,
Rekindling dreams once lost in space.
With each spark, a story unfolds,
Of love that breathes and never holds.

Through the ashes, we find our way,
A path of light that will not stray.
Holding tight to the fire's glow,
Together we rise, together we flow.

From depths forgotten, we will soar,
United now, forevermore.
The flame we nurture, fiercely bright,
Guides us forward into the night.

With every glance, the colors blend,
A symphony that will not end.
In the rekindled flame we trust,
Transforming dreams from ash to dust.

Breaths of a Burning Past

Echoes linger in silent halls,
Phantoms whisper 'neath brick walls.
Each fading memory, a silent cry,
As time flows swiftly, we wonder why.

The past, a fire that still remains,
With flickers bright, it leaves its stains.
Moments cherished, moments lost,
All bear witness to love's true cost.

In the embers, we seek the clue,
Breath of life in colors anew.
For what was once, will shape the now,
In the dance of time, we take a bow.

Through trials faced, we find our grace,
In every tear that leaves a trace.
The warmth of days we once embraced,
Kindles a fire that can't be replaced.

With every breath, we forge ahead,
Building journeys where hearts once bled.
In the burning past we'll find our way,
Embracing life in a brand new day.

Embers of Enterprise

Flickering light in the morning sun,
Ideas growing, a race begun.
In minds ignited, passions blaze,
Chasing dreams through a hopeful haze.

With every step, the vision clear,
As plans take hold, we persevere.
A dance of courage, we will dare,
Building bridges to lands so rare.

In the forge of life, we craft our fate,
Embers glowing, we will create.
Through every challenge, we rise and strive,
For in our hearts, the fire's alive.

With hands united, we draw the line,
Transforming dreams into something divine.
Together we rise, together we stand,
Creating futures that feel so grand.

With each ember, a spark of hope,
In enterprise, we learn to cope.
Fueled by passion, we'll sail the seas,
Embers of enterprise, hearts at ease.

Awakening the Molten Core

Deep inside, a whisper stirs,
Ancient rhythms, the heart prefers.
Molten magic flows through veins,
Awakening dreams, breaking chains.

From depths below, the fire calls,
Striking chords as the silence falls.
With every pulse, the world ignites,
Guided by stars on endless nights.

With courage fierce, we rise anew,
Dancing flames in a fiery hue.
As visions blend with the light of day,
We find the strength to lead the way.

In the core of every soul lies grace,
A molten heart in a timeless space.
Awakening now, we feel the burn,
Life's lessons taught, and we will learn.

Together we breathe, together we sing,
Embracing the fire that love will bring.
With open hearts, we journey on,
Awakening the core now brightly shone.

Life Unshackled

In chains no longer bound,
I dance beneath the sky.
With every step unbridled,
I feel my spirit fly.

The weight of past regrets,
Now lifted by the breeze.
I find my voice in freedom,
And let my heart's song tease.

Each moment now a treasure,
Unraveled in the light.
I embrace the unknown journey,
With courage and delight.

The shadows fade to whispers,
As dawn begins to break.
I rise with inner power,
With every choice I make.

In life unshackled, I stand tall,
A phoenix in the sun.
No chains can hold me captive,
My journey has begun.

The Glow of Renewal

In the quiet of the morning,
Hope awakens slow.
With tender hands of sunlight,
The earth begins to glow.

Once barren fields now flourish,
With colors bold and bright.
Each petal holds a promise,
A glimpse of pure delight.

The chill of night retreats now,
As warmth begins to spread.
New life emerges gently,
From every path once tread.

In moments lost to sorrow,
The heart begins to mend.
With every breath of springtime,
Old wounds begin to end.

The glow of renewal dances,
Across the waking land.
I find strength in the changes,
And rise to take my stand.

Rise Up and Roar

In shadows I have lingered,
But now I feel the fire.
With every ounce of courage,
I step toward my desire.

The whispers of the doubters,
No longer hold me back.
With strength like roaring thunder,
I blaze a fearless track.

With every breath of freedom,
I rise above the noise.
The world can feel my presence,
As I reclaim my voice.

The past won't keep me captive,
I shatter every chain.
With passion as my armor,
I triumph through the pain.

So hear me now, I'm rising,
A force you can't ignore.
In this moment, I am living—
I rise up and roar.

Sowing Seeds in the Ashes

In the remnants of old dreams,
I gather what is found.
With hope as my foundation,
New visions are unbound.

From ashes rise potential,
Each seed a story bold.
In barren ground, I nurture,
The future waits to unfold.

The pain of loss transforms me,
As grief turns into grace.
With every tear a blessing,
New life begins to place.

With sunlight as my ally,
I water all I've sown.
In fields once set to silence,
I've found my purpose grown.

So here I stand, unwavering,
Among the charred remains.
With love, I plant my courage,
As growth breaks through the chains.

Resurrection Reverie

In the shadows, whispers call,
Life awakens, heeds the thrall.
Silent murmurs weave through night,
Hope reborn in dawning light.

Petals gleam with morning dew,
Fragrant sighs of colors new.
Every heartbeat, soft and slow,
Beneath the earth, the dreams still grow.

From ashes rise the tales of old,
Stories waiting to be told.
Through the pain, the strength we gain,
In this reverie, we remain.

Stars align, a cosmic dance,
Graced by fate, we take our chance.
With each breath, the world expands,
In unity, our story stands.

Awake, arise, the time is near,
In resurrection, cast aside fear.
The journey's start, the end unknown,
In every heart, a seed is sown.

Flames and Fragments

In the night, the embers glow,
Flickering tales of long ago.
Rising smoke, a haunting song,
Memories where we all belong.

Fragments dance in the fiery light,
Bitter truth in the blackest night.
With every spark, a story burns,
Lessons learned, the wheel still turns.

Through the chaos, beauty blooms,
In the ashes, life resumes.
Each tiny flame, a fight to keep,
In the dark, our spirits leap.

Casting shadows, flickers fade,
Yet in the night, the dreams cascade.
With courage, let our hearts ignite,
Transform the fragments into light.

Rising from the heat of pain,
Strength and hope we shall regain.
In this dance of fire and fate,
We forge our path, we liberate.

Scorched Paths to Growth

Beneath the sun, the earth does crack,
Scorched and bare, there's no turning back.
Yet through the flames, the seeds take root,
In barren soil, resilience shoots.

Nature sighs, a weary breath,
Through trials faced, we learn of death.
Yet from the ashes, greens unfold,
A testament to stories bold.

Footprints marked by tears and sweat,
In every struggle, no regret.
Growth emerges from charred remains,
With every bruise, a lesson gained.

In the light of the setting sun,
New beginnings have just begun.
With every scar that we amass,
We find our strength; we rise at last.

Through scorched paths, we boldly tread,
With hearts ignited, we are led.
To forge a way through pain and strife,
In every struggle, we find life.

Heart of the Ember

Within the dark, a spark ignites,
A hidden flame in endless nights.
With gentle warmth, it guides the way,
Through shadows long, to brighter day.

In whispered winds, the embers call,
Reminders sweet of rise and fall.
In stillness found, our hearts embrace,
Echoes of love, a sacred space.

Fires dance in the silent air,
Each flicker tells of hope, of care.
In the glow, our fears take flight,
Together we ignite the light.

Through trials faced, we stand as one,
In the struggle, we've just begun.
With each heartbeat, passions blend,
In the heart of embers, we transcend.

Let our spirits soar and dream,
In unity, we build the beam.
Burning bright, our souls entwined,
A legacy of love enshrined.

The Unseen Flourish

In shadows deep, the roots do weave,
A world alive, we can't perceive.
Beneath the earth, where silence grows,
The unseen flair of life bestows.

In hidden nooks, the whispers hum,
A gentle dance, where dreams can come.
Though light is faint, and hope seems far,
Within the dark, they rise like stars.

With every drop of rain that falls,
The silent blooms break earthly walls.
Emerging soft, they greet the day,
In every shade, they find their way.

In twilight's glow, they stretch and reach,
Life's quiet lesson, nature's teach.
Each petal opens, a tale retold,
In colors bright, their hearts are bold.

So let us pause, and gently see,
The unseen flourish, wild and free.
In every breath, a pulse anew,
A world alive, begins with you.

The Quiet Return

When autumn leaves begin to fall,
In whispered hues, they heed the call.
The silence wraps the earth in grace,
A quiet hush, a soft embrace.

The rivers slow, the skies turn gray,
Yet life still breathes beneath the clay.
In stillness blooms a tender shoot,
The heartbeats strong, the roots take root.

As winter's chill coats all in white,
The promise of spring, a hopeful sight.
Beneath the frost, the seeds reside,
In quietude, they bide their time.

When longer days return once more,
And warmth rekindles every shore,
The quiet strength will rise again,
In vibrant hues, through sun and rain.

So let us trust the cycle's flow,
In every end, a chance to grow.
The quiet return, a timeless theme,
In nature's heart, we find the dream.

Scorched Earth

Beneath the sun's relentless blaze,
The land now bears the fiery haze.
As embers fade and ash takes flight,
A canvas gray, devoid of light.

The cracks in soil, so deep and wide,
Where once there danced the lush green tide.
Yet in this blackened, barren scene,
Lies hope concealed, though seldom seen.

For from the depths of darkness' clutch,
The seeds of life will always touch.
In hardened ground, a flicker sparks,
Resilience blooms in hidden arcs.

When rains return, and clouds align,
The earth will sing, her heart divine.
With every drop, the healing starts,
Reviving life, forgiving hearts.

So fear not flames, nor scorched despair,
For nature's strength is always there.
Through fire and ash, a tale reborn,
A vibrant dawn, a bright new morn.

Flourishing Seeds

In pockets soft, the seeds await,
The tender touch of love and fate.
With dreams entwined, their spirits rise,
To kiss the sun and paint the skies.

Each hidden gem, a world unknown,
Within the soil, they've gently grown.
Their whispered hopes, in shadows kept,
In silence loud, their secrets swept.

And when the winds of chance do call,
They break the ground, defy the fall.
With every sunbeam's warm embrace,
They burst alive, reclaim their space.

In vibrant colors, they unite,
A tapestry of pure delight.
The flourishing seeds, a testament,
To nature's love, so freely spent.

So let us cherish every sprout,
In every heart, a life about.
The flourishing seeds, a gift to see,
In every breath, we find the key.

The Symphony of Smolder

In twilight's haze, the embers glint,
A symphony of smoke and tint.
The fire's hush, a soulful song,
Where warmth and loss have both belonged.

Each crackle sparks a memory,
Of moments passed, now set free.
With every sigh, the flames embrace,
The beauty found in time and space.

The shadows dance upon the ground,
In whispering winds, old tales abound.
Yet in the fade, new light will glow,
From ashes deep, the seeds will grow.

Through smoldered past, our hearts will ache,
Yet in the pain, a bond we make.
For in this symphony, we hear,
The echoes sweet, both far and near.

So let us cherish all we've lost,
For in the flames, we find the cost.
The symphony of smolder sings,
A tale of life, of fragile things.

Rise Like the Sun

In the dawn's gentle embrace,
Golden rays start to chase.
Night's shadows fade away,
Hope blooms with a brand new day.

Warming hearts that were cold,
Stories of courage unfold.
Every moment a gift,
In the light, spirits lift.

Dreams awaken with light,
Chasing away the night.
Beneath an endless sky,
Live bold and never shy.

As horizons turn bright,
We chase our fears from sight.
Together we stand strong,
In unity, we belong.

With each sunrise we find,
The strength to be kind.
So rise, oh wanderer,
Let your heart's fire stir.

Shadows Give Way to Radiance

In the stillness of night,
Shadows whisper, take flight.
But dawn is breaking near,
Illuminating what we fear.

Each ghostly form retreats,
As light dances, it greets.
Whispers of hope resound,
In the warmth, love is found.

The past may seek to bind,
Yet the future is kind.
With every ray that beams,
We awaken our dreams.

The heart learns to trust,
In the rising dust.
From shadows we depart,
With brightness in our heart.

Together let us shine,
In a world that's divine.
For shadows never stay,
When radiance leads the way.

Threads of Hope

In the fabric of our days,
Woven with love's soft gaze.
Threads of hope intertwined,
In every soul, they bind.

Though storms may tear apart,
Resilience fills the heart.
With each fragile strand,
We find strength in our hand.

Colors of faith and grace,
Stitching time and place.
Every tear we mend,
Brings a brighter end.

Together we create,
A tapestry of fate.
In unity we trust,
Uplifted from the dust.

So hold on to the thread,
That life's journey we tread.
For woven in our fears,
Are the dreams of all years.

Where Phoenix Feet Tread

In the ashes, we begin,
Rising strong from within.
With every step we take,
New life begins to wake.

Flames of change ignite the night,
In their glow, we find our light.
With wings that soar and spread,
We create where others dread.

Embrace the fire's dance,
In its warmth, take a chance.
From the past, we have fled,
Into futures that we've bred.

Where hope and strength combine,
A journey that's divine.
So let your spirit rise,
Under vast, open skies.

For where phoenix feet tread,
Love and courage are bred.
In every heart's desire,
We find strength in the fire.